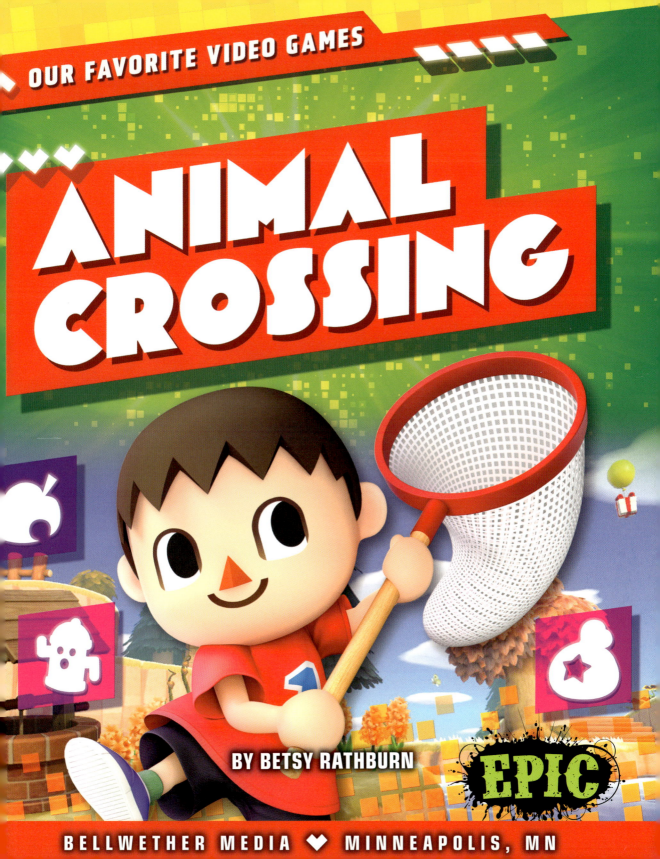

EPIC

EPIC BOOKS are no ordinary books. They burst with intense action, high-speed heroics, and shadows of the unknown. Are you ready for an Epic adventure?

This is not an official Animal Crossing book. It is not approved by or connected with Nintendo.

This edition first published in 2026 by Bellwether Media, Inc.

No part of this publication may be reproduced in whole or in part without written permission of the publisher. For information regarding permission, write to Bellwether Media, Inc., Attention: Permissions Department, 3500 American Blvd W, Suite 150, Bloomington, MN 55431.

Library of Congress Cataloging-in-Publication Data

Names: Rathburn, Betsy, author.
Title: Animal crossing / by Betsy Rathburn.
Description: Minneapolis, MN : Bellwether Media, 2026. | Series: Epic. Our favorite video games | Includes bibliographical references and index. | Audience term: juvenile | Audience: Ages 7-12 Bellwether Media | Audience: Grades 4-6 Bellwether Media | Summary: "Engaging images accompany information about the video game Animal Crossing. The combination of high-interest subject matter and light text is intended for students in grades 2 through 7"-- Provided by publisher.
Identifiers: LCCN 2025003637 (print) | LCCN 2025003638 (ebook) | ISBN 9798893045055 (library binding) | ISBN 9798893047349 (paperback) | ISBN 9798893046434 (ebook)
Subjects: LCSH: Animal Crossing video games--Juvenile literature.
Classification: LCC GV1469.35.A67 R37 2026 (print) | LCC GV1469.35.A67 (ebook) | DDC 794.8--dc23/eng/20250220
LC record available at https://lccn.loc.gov/2025003637
LC ebook record available at https://lccn.loc.gov/2025003638

Text copyright © 2026 by Bellwether Media, Inc. EPIC and associated logos are trademarks and/or registered trademarks of Bellwether Media, Inc. Bellwether Media is a division of FlutterBee Education Group.

Editor: Christina Leaf   Designer: Gabriel Hilger

Printed in the United States of America, North Mankato, MN.

TABLE OF CONTENTS

BUILDING UP 4

THE HISTORY OF ANIMAL CROSSING 8

ANIMAL CROSSING TODAY 16

ANIMAL CROSSING FANS 20

GLOSSARY 22

TO LEARN MORE 23

INDEX 24

000
HIGH SCORE

BUILDING UP

A player sells a load of fish to Nook's Cranny. Now they have enough Bells to **upgrade** their house.

They head to Town Hall to talk to Tom Nook. He will build a new room!

MORE BELLS!

In *Animal Crossing: New Horizons*, players must pay 5,696,000 Bells to fully upgrade their home!

ANIMAL CROSSING: NEW HORIZONS

TOM NOOK

5

Animal Crossing is a **series** of **simulation games**. Players explore a town or island. They become friends with animal characters.

They sell bugs, fish, and fruit to earn Bells. They can **decorate** their house and buy clothes!

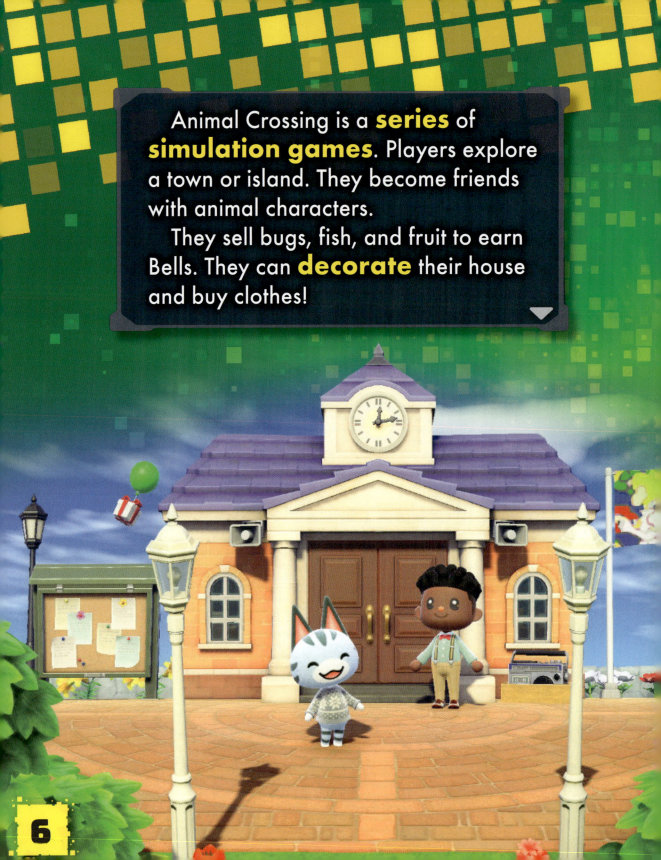

ANIMAL CROSSING FRUIT

APPLE

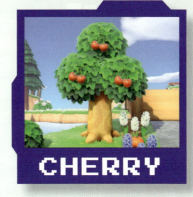
CHERRY

COCONUT

ORANGE

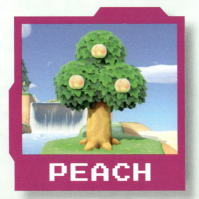
PEACH

PEAR

THE HISTORY OF ANIMAL CROSSING

The first Animal Crossing game came out in 2001. It was called *Dōbutsu no Mori*. It was only released in Japan.

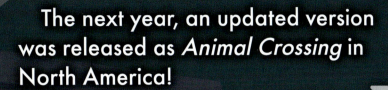

The next year, an updated version was released as *Animal Crossing* in North America!

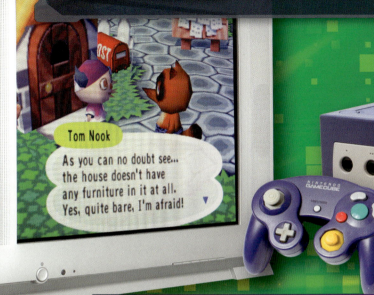

DEVELOPER PROFILE

NAME	Nintendo
LOCATION	Kyoto, Japan
YEAR FOUNDED	1889
NUMBER OF EMPLOYEES	8,109 in 2024

9

Animal Crossing: Wild World came out in 2005. This **sequel** was released for the Nintendo DS.

DIFFERENT EVERY DAY

Animal Crossing games follow the time in real life. There are days and nights. The seasons change, too!

NINTENDO DS

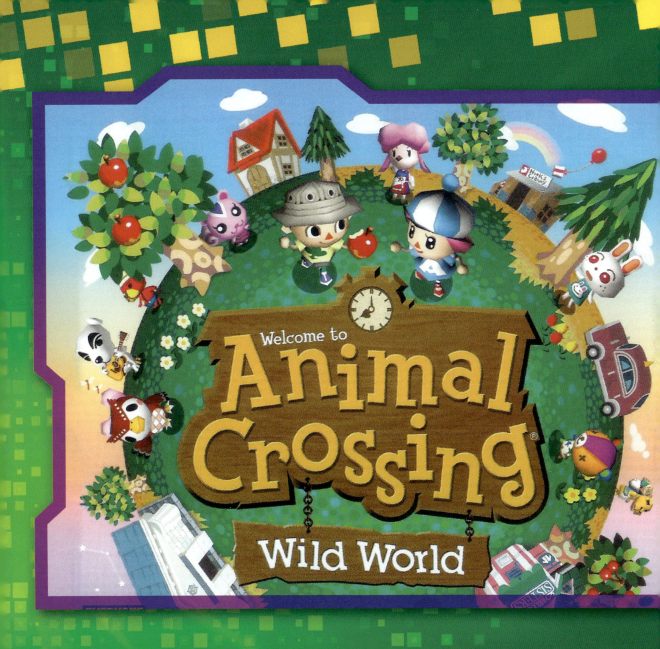

Players could connect online. This let them visit their friends' villages. Over 11 million copies sold!

In 2008, Animal Crossing: City Folk was released for the Wii.

ANIMAL CROSSING: CITY FOLK

NINTENDO WII

Four years later, *Animal Crossing: New Leaf* came out for the Nintendo 3DS. In this game, the player is their new town's mayor!

ANIMAL CROSSING: NEW LEAF

NINTENDO 3DS

ANIMAL CROSSING: NEW HORIZONS

In 2020, *Animal Crossing: New Horizons* became the best-selling Animal Crossing game. Players move to an island. They can **customize** their island and home. Over 47 million copies have been sold!

ANIMAL CROSSING TIMELINE

2001
Dōbutsu no Mori is released for the Nintendo 64 in Japan

2002
Animal Crossing is released for the GameCube in North America

2005
Animal Crossing: Wild World is released for the Nintendo DS

2008
Animal Crossing: City Folk is released for the Wii

2012
Animal Crossing: New Leaf is released for the Nintendo 3DS

2020
Animal Crossing: New Horizons is released for the Nintendo Switch

ANIMAL CROSSING TODAY

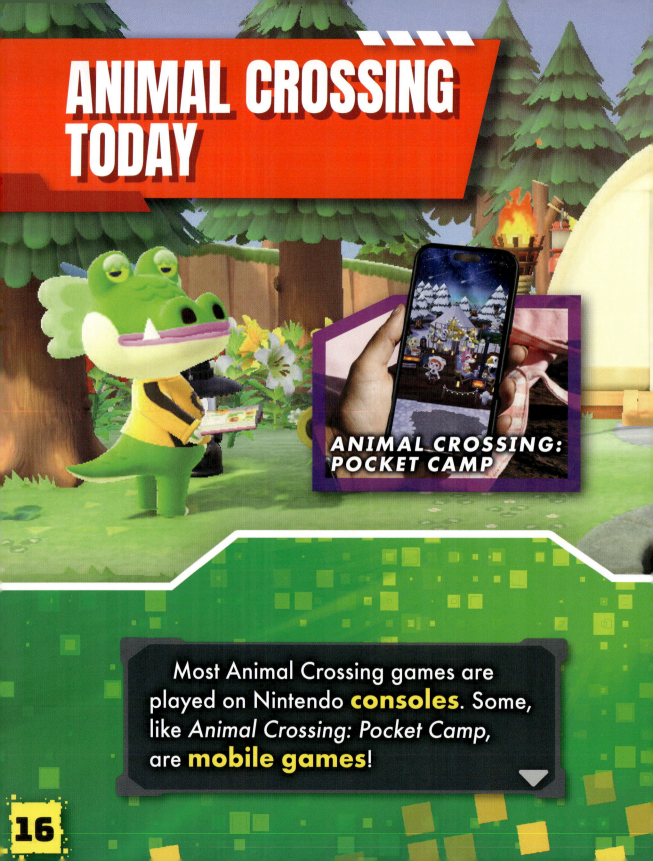

ANIMAL CROSSING: POCKET CAMP

Most Animal Crossing games are played on Nintendo **consoles**. Some, like *Animal Crossing: Pocket Camp*, are **mobile games**!

HOLIDAY FUN!

Animal Crossing games have many fun holidays. Players can collect special items and attend events!

Players become friends with animal neighbors. They talk to and visit their friends.

Players collect furniture and clothing. They go fishing or catch bugs. They can even create custom **designs**!

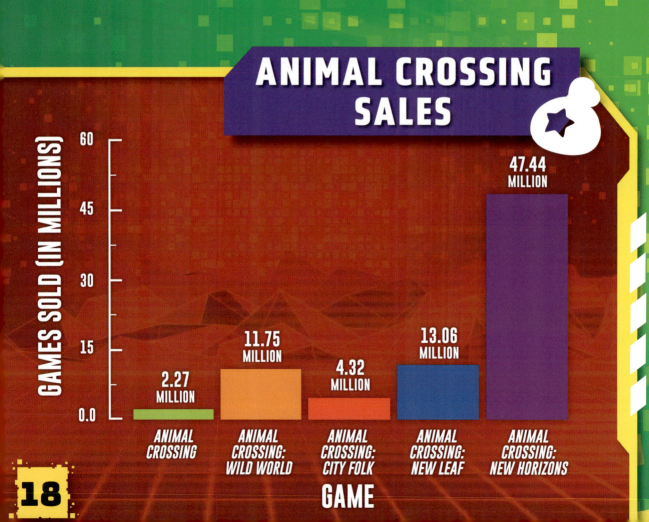

ANIMAL CROSSING SALES

- Animal Crossing: 2.27 million
- Animal Crossing: Wild World: 11.75 million
- Animal Crossing: City Folk: 4.32 million
- Animal Crossing: New Leaf: 13.06 million
- Animal Crossing: New Horizons: 47.44 million

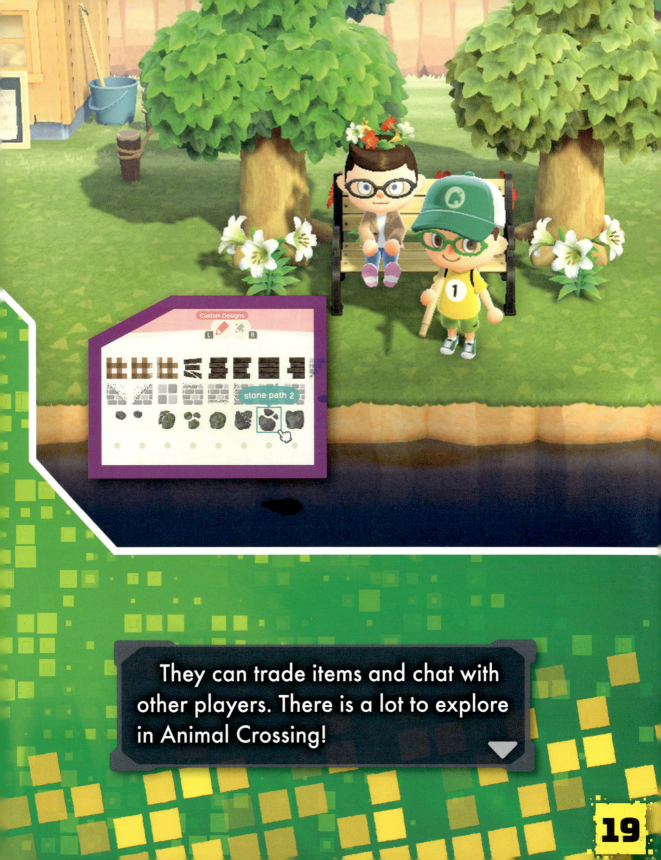

They can trade items and chat with other players. There is a lot to explore in Animal Crossing!

ANIMAL CROSSING FANS

Fans can enjoy the game in the real world. Some **aquariums** have hosted *Animal Crossing: New Horizons* events. Fans can collect real-life items, too. LEGO sets are popular. There are many ways to have fun with Animal Crossing!

ANIMAL CROSSING LEGO SET

NAME
Isabelle's House Visit

RELEASED
March 1, 2024

NUMBER OF PIECES
389

GLOSSARY

aquariums—places where animals that live in water are kept and shown

consoles—game systems that connect to TVs to play video games

customize—to make based on personal preferences

decorate—to make something look nice by adding beautiful things

designs—patterns or drawings made for clothing or furniture

mobile games—games that can be played almost anywhere on devices such as smartphones

sequel—a work that continues the story of a previous work

series—a number of related games

simulation games—games made to be like real life

upgrade—to make something better

TO LEARN MORE

AT THE LIBRARY

Downs, Kieran. *Super Mario Bros.* Minneapolis, Minn.: Bellwether Media, 2025.

Galanin, Dennis. *The Amazing World of Video Game Development.* Sanger, Calif.: Familius, 2022.

Shaw, Gina. *What Is Nintendo?* New York, N.Y.: Penguin Workshop, 2021.

ON THE WEB

FACTSURFER

Factsurfer.com gives you a safe, fun way to find more information.

1. Go to www.factsurfer.com.

2. Enter "Animal Crossing" into the search box and click 🔍.

3. Select your book cover to see a list of related content.

INDEX

Animal Crossing, 9

Animal Crossing: City Folk, 12

Animal Crossing: New Horizons, 5, 14, 20

Animal Crossing: New Leaf, 13

Animal Crossing: Pocket Camp, 16

Animal Crossing: Wild World, 10

aquariums, 20

Bells, 4, 5, 6

bugs, 6, 18

characters, 4, 5, 6, 17

consoles, 10, 12, 13, 16

Dōbutsu no Mori, 8

fans, 20

fish, 6, 18

fruit, 6, 7

history, 8, 9, 10, 11, 12, 13, 14, 15

holidays, 17

house, 4, 5, 6, 14

Japan, 8

LEGO sets, 20

mobile games, 16

Nintendo, 9, 16

Nook, Tom, 4, 5

North America, 9

player, 4, 5, 6, 11, 13, 14, 17, 18, 19

sales, 11, 14, 18

seasons, 10

simulation games, 6

time, 10

timeline, 15

The images in this book are reproduced through the courtesy of: Jae Yoon Park/ Flickr, front cover; Gabriel Hilger, pp. 3, 5 (all), 6, 7 (all), 13, 15 (2002, 2008, 2012, 2020), 16-17, 17 (holiday fun), 19 (all), 21; Nicole Lienemann/ AdobeStock, p. 4; ArcadeImages/ Alamy Stock Photo, pp. 8 (all), 9 (*Animal Crossing*); Igor Bronislavovich/ AdobeStock, p. 9 (TV); CTR Photos, p. 9 (GameCube); seeshooteatrepeat, p. 9 (GameCube controller); HauLar, p. 9 (Nintendo headquarters); finix_observer/ AdobeStock, p. 10 (Nintendo DS); L ke/ Wikipedia, p. 10 (*Animal Crossing: Wild World* gameplay); Brittany McIntosh, pp. 10 (different every day), 14 (all), 16 (*Animal Crossing: Pocket Camp*); Zxcvbnm/ Wikipedia, pp. 11, 15 (2005); Results May Vary/ Wikipedia, p. 12 (*Animal Crossing: City Folk*); YOSHIKAZU TSUNO/ Staff/ Getty Images, p. 12 (Nintendo Wii); Diego/ AdobeStock, p. 16 (inset); Ellianne, p. 20; miles_around/ AdobeStock, p. 21 (bottom inset); B.O'Kane/ Alamy Stock Photo, p. 21 (top inset); Michael San Diego, p. 22; Rafael Elias Henrique, p. 22 (Tom Nook); Tinxi, p. 23.